About Skill Builders
Algebra
Grades 6–8

Welcome to Skill Builders *Algebra* for grades 6–8. This book is designed to reinforce abstract mathematical thinking through focused practice. This full-color workbook contains grade-level-appropriate activities based on national standards to help ensure that children master basic skills before progressing.

More than 70 pages of activities cover essential algebraic skills, including exponents, expressions and equations, integers and rational numbers, working with inequalities, factoring, quadratic equations, graphing, and linear equations. The book's colorful, inviting format, easy-to-follow directions, and clear examples help build children's confidence and make algebra more accessible and enjoyable.

The Skill Builders series offers workbooks that are perfect for keeping skills sharp during the school year or preparing students for the next grade.

www.carsondellosa.com
Carson-Dellosa Publishing LLC
Greensboro, North Carolina

ISBN 978-1-936023-15-8
05-063131151

Table of Contents

Exponential Notation

Evaluate each expression.

Example:

$$(2x)^3 \text{ if } x = 2$$

$$(2 \bullet 2)^3 = 4^3 = \textbf{64}$$

Note: $\bullet$ means *multiply*

1. y^3 if $y = 5$

2. m^1 if $m = 21$

3. $3n^5$ if $n = 2$

4. $(3n)^5$ if $n = 2$

5. $x^3 - 5$ if $x = 2$

6. $3y^4 + 5$ if $y = 3$

7. $x^2 y$ if $x = 4$, $y = 5$

8. $c^2 + c$ if $c = 5$

9. $5xy^2$ if $x = 5$, $y = 2$

10. $4m^0$ if $m = 5$

Writing Algebraic Expressions

Write each phrase as an algebraic expression.

> **Example:**
>
> 4 less than a number
> **$n - 4$**

1. 5 more than x

2. c less than 5

3. p added to 10

4. the product of 3 and h

5. half of y

6. three times a number

7. a number increased by three times y

8. a number y increased by itself

9. three less than twice y

10. 2 more than the product of 6 and y

11. the quotient of a number divided by 10

12. the perimeter of a square with sides length s

Solving Equations Using Addition and Subtraction

Solve each equation.

Example:

$$y + 57 = 119$$
$$y = 119 - 57$$
$$\mathbf{y = 62}$$

1. $y + 2.6 = 9.8$

2. $m - 37 = 312$

3. $a - 12 = 101$

4. $y + 89 = 376$

5. $c + 2.04 = 3.68$

6. $y - 1{,}064 = 3{,}882$

7. $a + \dfrac{2}{7} = \dfrac{6}{7}$

8. $p - \dfrac{4}{15} = \dfrac{3}{5}$

9. $6.44 = y + 1.78$

10. $23 = y - 261$

Solving Equations Using Multiplication and Division

Solve each equation.

Example:

$$9m = 108$$
$$m = \frac{108}{9}$$
$$\mathbf{m = 12}$$

1. $26m = 182$

2. $102 = 17c$

3. $\dfrac{x}{0.11} = 6$

4. $\dfrac{m}{6} = 62$

5. $3p = 183$

6. $5.44 = 0.34a$

7. $59 = \dfrac{x}{4}$

8. $\dfrac{r}{0.2} = 4.8$

9. $23y = 115$

10. $9m = 3.6$

Using Equations to Solve Problems

Solve each problem by writing an equation.

1. The product of a number and 7 is 63.

2. An independent contractor charges $60 per hour. How many hours did the contractor work to make $42,720?

3. Mariah paid $5.00 for a dozen bagels. About how much does one bagel cost?

4. Nadia scored a 75 on her second math test. That was 12 points less than her score on the first math test. What was her score on the first test?

5. There are 324 golf balls on the driving range. If half of them are white, how many white golf balls are there?

6. Michael has saved $56.25. He wants to buy a pair of $70 shoes. How much more money does he need to save?

Integers

Evaluate.

Example:

The **absolute value** of a number is its distance from zero on a number line.

|-3| = **3** because -3 is 3 places from zero.

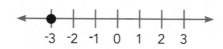

1. |-35|

2. |6.8|

3. |-4| + |-5|

4. |13| + |-13|

5. |-8| • |-2|

6. |-5| • |-7| • |0|

Order from least to greatest.

Example:

15, -21, -15 = **-21, -15, 15**

7. 14, -13, 6, -16

8. -33, 5, 0, -18

9. -34, -36, -28, -32, -4

10. 14, -24, -14, -6, 6

Using the Distributive Property

Simplify.

Example:

Multiply the term outside the parentheses by each term inside the parentheses.

$$8(y - 4) = 8y - 8(4)$$
$$= 8y - 32$$

1. $7(x - 7)$

2. $-5(y - 4)$

3. $3(x - 2y)$

4. $-4(x - 2y + 3)$

5. $6(3x - 4y + 8z)$

6. $2.1(-1.2x + 2.3y - 1.1)$

7. $-8(3x + 2y - 6)$

8. $3(4a - 5b + 7)$

9. $\frac{2}{3}(6x - 9y)$

10. $\frac{-5}{6}(x - \frac{1}{2}y + 12)$

Combining Like Terms

Combine the like terms.

Example:

$$4x + 5y - 6x - 2y = 4x - 6x + 5y - 2y$$

$$= (4 - 6)x + (5 - 2)y$$

$$= \textbf{-2x + 3y}$$

1. $5y - y$

2. $x - 4x$

3. $3a + 2a$

4. $m - 0.5m$

5. $11x + 3y - 5x$

6. $6y + 3z - 3y$

7. $13a - 13b - 13c + 15a$

8. $6p + 2p - 18$

9. $\frac{2}{5}y + \frac{3}{5}x + \frac{1}{5}y - \frac{2}{5}x$

10. $17a + 18b - 20b + a$

Simplifying Algebraic Expressions

Simplify each algebraic expression.

Example:

$$4a - 3 - (2a - 5) = 4a - 3 - 2a + 5$$
$$= 4a - 2a - 3 + 5$$
$$\mathbf{= 2a + 2}$$

1. $6y - (3y + 10)$

2. $2x - (2x + 5)$

3. $4b - (6b - 8)$

4. $12m - (6m - 5)$

5. $2y + 8y - (6y + 12)$

6. $5x + 6x - (3x + 5)$

7. $3y - 4x - 2(4x - 5y)$

8. $6a - 3b + 2(b + 5a)$

9. $-(5a - 3x) - (3x - 5a)$

10. $(-6x + y) - (3y - 5x)$

Solving Two-Step Equations

Solve each equation.

Example:

$$-3x + 5 = 26$$

$$-3x + 5 - 5 = 26 - 5$$

$$\frac{-3x}{-3} = \frac{21}{-3}$$

$$x = -7$$

1. $7y + 9 = 72$

2. $4x - 6 = 38$

3. $7a + 2 = -47$

4. $5m + 4 = -51$

5. $-3x + 9 = -24$

6. $-6y - 18 = -84$

7. $-4x + 83 = -1$

8. $4 - 8m = 20$

9. $9y - 8 = -80$

10. $-18 - 3y = -57$

Solving Equations with Variables on Both Sides

Solve each equation.

Example:

$$3y - 3 = {}^-2y + 2$$
$$3y + 2y - 3 = {}^-2y + 2y + 2$$
$$5y - 3 = 2$$
$$5y - 3 + 3 = 2 + 3$$
$$5y = 5$$
$$\mathbf{y = 1}$$

1. $3m = 4m - 14$

2. $7x = 2x + 5$

3. $3x - 5 = 5 - 2x$

4. $2a - 1 = 4 + 5a$

5. $3b - 7b + 35 = 15 - 2b$

6. $20 - 3m = 2m - 8m + 50$

7. $6y - (3y + 9) = 17$

8. $3x - 10 = 5(x - 4)$

9. $3(y - 2) = 5(y + 2)$

10. $6(6n - 1) = 7(5n - 2)$

Solving Equations
Involving Absolute Value

Solve each equation.

Examples:

$$|x| + 3 = 14$$
$$|x| = 14 - 3$$
$$\mathbf{|x| = 11}$$

Since $|x| = 11$, both 11 and -11 could be substituted for x.

$$|x + 6| = 21$$
$$x + 6 = 21 \text{ or } x + 6 = -21$$

$$\mathbf{x = 15 \text{ or } x = -27}$$

1. $|m| - 6 = 1$

2. $3|x| + 2 = 17$

3. $5 + |x| = 23$

4. $6 + |m| - 10 = 3$

5. $-2|a| - 6 = -20$

6. $|7x - 3| = 4$

7. $|x - 10| = 6$

8. $|4n - 12| = 16$

9. $|8y + 3| = 21$

10. $5 + |2x - 1| = 8$

More Equations

Solve each equation.

1. $-8y + 3 = 35$

2. $6y + 9y = 45$

3. $4(3x + 2) = 56$

4. $20 - 2x = 30$

5. $6(3b - 2) + 5b = 57$

6. $5(m + 4) = 8(m - 2)$

7. $-2y + 11 = 6y - 13$

8. $2p - 6 - 6p = 10 - 2p + 4$

9. $-10 + 3|x| = 26$

10. $\frac{1}{2}m + \frac{1}{4} + \frac{3}{4}m = 1 + 2m$

11. $6 + |5y + 2| = 9$

12. $3|x + 3| = 15$

Finding Values of Functions

Find the following function values.

A **function** is a correspondence from one set to another. $f(x)$ is read "f of x". It does not mean f times x.

Examples:

Find $f(x) = 5x^2 - 3x + 1$ for the given value of x.

$x = -7$

$f(-7) = 5(-7)^2 - 3(-7) + 1$

$= 5(49) + 21 + 1$

$= 245 + 21 + 1$

$= \textbf{267}$

$x = 5a$

$f(5a) = 5(5a)^2 - 3(5a) + 1$

$= \textbf{125}a^2 - \textbf{15}a + \textbf{1}$

1. If $f(x) = 11x + 8x^2$

     a) $f(-6)$ b) $f(2)$ c) $f(-3)$ d) $f(1)$

2. If $g(x) = x^3$

     a) $g(-1)$ b) $g(4)$ c) $g(-5)$ d) $g(2m)$

3. If $h(x) = |x| + 2$

     a) $h(5)$ b) $h(-4)$ c) $h(-14)$ d) $h(x^2)$

Composite Functions

Find the composite of the following functions. Substitute the given expressions to solve.

Examples:

If $f(x) = x + 3$ and $g(x) = 2x^2$

When solving, substitute "$x + 3$" for $f(x)$. Substitute $2x^2$ for $g(x)$

Find $f(g(x))$.	Find $g(f(x))$.
Substitute $2x^2$ for $g(x)$ as given above.	Substitue "$x + 3$" for $f(x)$ as given above.
$f(g(x)) = f(2x^2)$ $= 2x^2 + 3$	$g(f(x)) = g(x + 3)$ $= 2(x + 3)^2$ $= 2(x^2 + 6x + 9)$ $= 2x^2 + 12x + 18$

$$f(x) = 3x - 5 \qquad g(x) = x^2 - 1 \qquad h(x) = x + 3$$

1. $f(g(x))$

2. $g(h(x))$

3. $h(f(x))$

4. $g(f(x))$

5. $f(h(x))$

6. $f(h(g(x)))$

Operations of Functions

Find the composite of the following functions. Substitute the given expressions to solve.

Examples:

If $f(x) = 3x + 4$ and $g(x) = x - 1$

Substitute the given expressions to solve.

Find $g(x) - f(x)$.

$g(x) - f(x) = x - 1 - (3x + 4)$

$= x - 1 - 3x - 4$

$= {}^{-}2x - 5$

Find $(f \bullet g)(x)$.

$(f \bullet g)(x) = (3x + 4)(x - 1)$

$= 3x^2 + x - 4$

$f(x) = 5x - 1$ $\qquad$ $g(x) = x^2 - 2$ $\qquad$ $h(x) = 3x$

1. $(f \bullet g)(x)$

2. $g(x) + h(x)$

3. $(g \bullet h)(x)$

4. $f(x) - g(x)$

5. $(f \bullet g)(3)$

6. $(g \bullet h)({}^{-}3)$

One-to-One Functions

Determine whether each graph is a function and 1-1.

A function must pass the vertical line test. A **1-1 function** passes both a vertical and a horizontal line test.

Example:

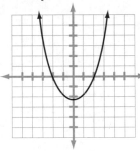

This graph passes the vertical line test because on any vertical line drawn, the graph only passes through the line once or not at all.

This graph does not pass the horizontal test because a horizontal line can be drawn that passes through more than one point.

This graph is a function, but not 1-1.

1.

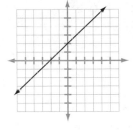

_____

2.

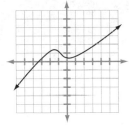

_____

3.

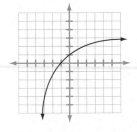

_____

4.

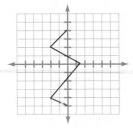

_____

Inverse Functions

Find the inverse of the following functions.

A function (f) has an inverse only if the function is 1-1. (It passes the vertical and horizontal line tests.) The inverse function is denoted as f-1.

Example:

Find the inverse of $f(x) = 2x + 8$.

1. Replace f(x) with y.
2. Interchange x and y.
3. Solve for y.

$$y = 2x + 8$$
$$x = 2y + 8$$
$$x - 8 = 2y$$
$$\frac{x}{2} - 4 = y$$
$$f^{-1}(x) = \frac{x}{2} - 4$$

1. $f(x) = 4x - 8$

2. $f(x) = 3x + 6$

3. $f(x) = \frac{x}{2} - 1$

4. $f(x) = (\frac{2}{3})x + 4$

5. $f(x) = \frac{4}{5x} - 3$

6. $f(x) = x^3$

Solving Formulas for a Variable

Solve each formula for the given variable.

Example:

$$A = bh \text{ for } b$$
$$\frac{A}{h} = \frac{bh}{h}$$
$$\frac{A}{h} = b$$

1. $d = rt$ for r

2. $d = rt$ for t

3. $I = prt$ for p

4. $I = prt$ for r

5. $A = \pi r^2$ for π

6. $A = \pi r^2$ for r^2

7. $P = 2l + 2w$ for w

8. $C = 2\pi r$ for r

9. $A = \frac{1}{2}bh$ for b

10. $E = mc^2$ for m

The Pythagorean Theorem

Find the missing side lengths. Round your answers to the nearest hundredth.

For a right triangle, the sum of the squares of the legs of the triangle equals the square of the hypotenuse. The **hypotenuse** is the side opposite the right angle.

In the triangle below, sides *a* and *b* are the legs of the triangle, while side c is the hypotenuse.

Example:

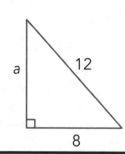

$$a^2 + b^2 = c^2$$
$$a^2 + 8^2 = 12^2$$
$$a^2 + 64 = 144$$
$$a^2 = 80$$
$$a = \sqrt{80}$$
$$a \approx 8.94$$

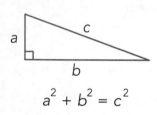 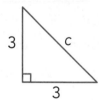

1. c = _____ 2. a = _____ 3. c = _____

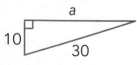 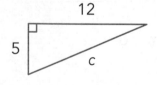 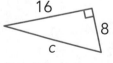

4. a = _____ 5. b = _____ 6. c = _____

Solving Inequalities Using Addition and Subtraction

Solve each inequality.

> **Example:**
>
> $$y - 6 \leq {}^-10$$
> $$y \leq {}^-10 + 6$$
> $$\mathbf{y \leq {}^-4}$$

1. $x + 5 > 12$

2. $y + 9 \leq {}^-12$

3. $a + 30 < 11$

4. $m - 9 \geq {}^-9$

5. $x - 15 > {}^-16$

6. $b - 2.5 \leq 6.7$

7. $m + \dfrac{1}{3} < \dfrac{4}{9}$

8. $c - \dfrac{1}{4} \geq \dfrac{1}{4}$

9. $\dfrac{2}{3} + x < \dfrac{4}{9}$

10. $5m - 4m < 21$

Solving Inequalities Using Multiplication and Division

Solve each inequality.

Examples:

When multiplying or dividing by a negative number, remember to reverse the inequality symbol.

$$-4x < 20$$
$$\frac{-4x}{-4} > \frac{20}{-4}$$
$$x > -5$$

$$5m > -3$$
$$\frac{5m}{5} > \frac{-3}{5}$$
$$m > \frac{-3}{5}$$

1. $6x \geq -24$

2. $-4m < 32$

3. $-5y \leq -25$

4. $20p > -400$

5. $-x < \dfrac{1}{4}$

6. $-3y \geq \dfrac{3}{8}$

7. $9x \leq -6.3$

8. $27 < -10n + n$

Solving Multistep Inequalities

Solve each inequality.

Example:

$$6 - 8x \geq 3 - 9x$$
$$6 - 8x + 9x \geq 3$$
$$6 + x \geq 3$$
$$x \geq 3 - 6$$
$$\mathbf{x \geq \text{-}3}$$

1. $6 + 8x \leq 46$

2. $\text{-}3x - 5 > 13$

3. $6 - 5y \geq 21$

4. $\text{-}7x + 4 < 39$

5. $19 - 6m - 2m > 39$

6. $10a + 7 - 7a \leq \text{-}6$

7. $28 - 10x > 15x - 17$

8. $43 - 14b < 14b - 13$

9. $\dfrac{\text{-}3m}{5} < \text{-}15$

10. $\dfrac{x}{4} + 1 \geq \dfrac{1}{4}$

Graphing Inequalities on a Number Line

Solve and graph the solution on a number line.

Example:

$x - 6 \leq -7$
$x \leq$ -1

For $\leq$ or $\geq$, use a solid circle. For $<$ or $>$, use an open circle.

1. $y + 5 > 14$

2. $6x \leq 30$

3. $^-9c - 12 \leq 42$

4. $7m + 4 \geq 25$

Multiplying Using Exponents

Simplify. Write using exponents.

Examples:

$$6^2 \cdot 6^5 = 6^{2+5} = \mathbf{6^7} \qquad \Big| \qquad x^2 \cdot y^3 \cdot x^2 = x^{2+2} \cdot y^3 = \mathbf{x^4 y^3}$$

1. $3^5 \cdot 3^4$

2. $9^9 \cdot 9^5 \cdot 9$

3. $(-5)^4(-5)^3$

4. $x^3 \cdot x^{10}$

5. $y^8 \cdot y^0 \cdot y^5$

6. $m \cdot m \cdot m$

7. $(x^2 y^5)(x^3 y^5)$

8. $(3a^4 b^5)(3a^2 b^3)$

9. $(b^2 c^5 d)(b^5 cd)$

10. $(2xy^3)(2x^3 y)$

11. $(mn^4)(m^5 n^6)$

12. $(xyz)(x^3 y^2 z^4)$

Dividing Using Exponents

Simplify. Write using exponents.

Examples:

$$\frac{5^5}{5^2} = 5^{5-2} = \mathbf{5^3}$$

$$\frac{x^6}{x} = x^{6-1} = \mathbf{x^5}$$

1. $\dfrac{6^7}{6^3}$

2. $\dfrac{4^9}{4^5}$

3. $\dfrac{n^6}{n^5}$

4. $\dfrac{x^{10}}{x^7}$

5. $\dfrac{a^4}{a}$

6. $\dfrac{m^5 n^7}{mn^4}$

7. $\dfrac{a^9 b}{a^8 b}$

8. $\dfrac{4^4 x^5}{4^3 x^2}$

9. $\dfrac{x^4 y^3}{xy}$

10. $\dfrac{5^2 a^4 b}{5a^2 b}$

Exponents

Express using positive exponents.

Examples:

$$a^{-2} = \frac{1}{a^2}$$

$$xy^{-1} = x \cdot \frac{1}{y} = \frac{x}{y}$$

1. 4^{-3}

2. 5^{-4}

3. m^{-6}

4. $(3y)^{-2}$

5. $7n^{-4}$

6. cd^{-5}

Simplify.

Example:

$$(2x^3)^2 = 2^2(x^3)^2$$

$$= 4x^6$$

7. $(4^2)^2$

8. $(m^4)^8$

9. $(2t)^4$

10. $(3x^2)^3$

11. $(\frac{2}{a^2})^2$

12. $(\frac{ab^2}{c})^3$

Multiplying Monomials

Multiply.

Example:

$$(\text{-}5a^2b^3)(4ab^2) = (\text{-}5 \bullet 4)(a^2 \bullet a)(b^3 \bullet b^2)$$
$$= \textbf{-20}a^3b^5$$

1. $(4y)(\text{-}3)$

2. $\text{-}x(x)$

3. $(\text{-}m)(\text{-}m)$

4. $(4p^2)(2p^5)$

5. $(\text{-}y^3)(y^5)$

6. $(\text{-}6n^2)(\text{-}5n^4)$

7. $(a^3b^4)(a^2b)$

8. $(\text{-}3xy^3)(9x^3y^2)$

9. $(4m^4n)(\text{-}4m^2n^5)$

10. $(8c^2)(2c)(\text{-}3c^3)$

Dividing Monomials

Divide.

Example:

$$\frac{6x^4y^5}{-3x^2y} = \frac{6}{-3} \cdot x^{4-2} \cdot y^{5-1}$$

$$= -2x^2y^2$$

1. $\dfrac{m^7}{m^4}$

2. $\dfrac{12x^2}{8x}$

3. $\dfrac{b^6}{b}$

4. $\dfrac{4c^3}{c^6}$

5. $\dfrac{-8x^{10}}{2x^5}$

6. $\dfrac{16y^2}{-4y^2}$

7. $\dfrac{-35m^5}{35}$

8. $\dfrac{32x^6y^8}{-4x^6y^3}$

9. $\dfrac{5m^{10}n^6}{-7m^5n^2}$

10. $\dfrac{36a^6b^3}{-9ab^3}$

Polynomials

Simplify.

Example:

$$4a^5b^3 + 3ab^2 - 2a^5b^3 - 5ab^2$$

$$= (4-2)a^5b^3 + (3-5)ab^2$$

$$= \mathbf{2a^5b^3 - 2ab^2}$$

1. $2y - 5y^3 - 32 - 8y^3$

2. $8n^3 - n - n^3 - 8$

3. $6y^2 + 5y^2 - 4$

4. $4c^4 - 2c + 2c + c^4$

5. $7x^3 + 6xy^2 - 2x^3 - 3xy^2$

6. $-9a^2b^2 + 3ab - 6a^2b^2 - 5ab$

7. $3xy^2 + 4xy - 10xy^2 + xy$

8. $3m^2n^2 - m^2 + m^3 - 2 - 2m^2n^2$

9. $4x^2y + xy - 4x^2y - xy + 3x^2y$

Adding Polynomials

Add.

Example:

$$(2x^3 - 3x - 5) + (4x^3 - 2x^2 + 3)$$

$$= 2x^3 - 3x - 5 + 4x^3 - 2x^2 + 3$$

$$= \mathbf{6x^3 - 2x^2 - 3x - 2}$$

1. $(-2a^2 + 5a) + (3a^2 + a)$

2. $(32y^4 + y^2 + 3y) + (3y^2 - 2y)$

3. $(4m^5 + 7m^2 - 1) + (6m^2 + 5m - 2)$

4. $(-5x^3 + 7x^2 - 2x - 1) + (4x^3 + 3x - 9)$

5. $(10x^7 - 8x^4 + 3x^2 + 2) + (6x^5 - 2x^4 + 5x^2)$

6. $(-2m^4n^3 + 7m^3n^3 - 5m^2 + 2mn^2 + 3) + (-m^3n^3 + 3m^2 + 6)$

Subtracting Polynomials

Subtract.

Example:

$$(8y^2 + 6) - (5y^2 + 2) = 8y^2 + 6 - 5y^2 - 2$$
$$= 3y^2 + 4$$

1. $(4a^4 + 5) - (2a^4 - 1)$

2. $(\text{-}5x^3 + 3x + 7) - (\text{-}4x^2 - 5)$

3. $(8y^3 - 3y + 9) - (8y^2 + 2y - 7)$

4. $9m^3 - (\text{-}3m^2 - 2m + 1)$

5. $(6x^4 - 2x^3 + 3x + 1) - (3x^3 - 2x + 5)$

6. $(6t^4 + 5t) - (5t^5 - 2t^4 + 3t^2 + 2t - 1)$

7. $(y^4 - 2y^2 + y + 1) - (y^4 - 3y^3 + 3y - 1)$

8. $(5n^5 + 2n^3 + 6n - 3) - (4n^5 - 5n^4 - 8n - 6)$

9. $(6ab^5 + b^4 - 4ab^3 + 2b^2) - (\text{-}ab^5 - ab^4 - b^2 - 1)$

Multiplying Monomials

Multiply.

Example:

$$3x(4x + 5) = (3x)(4x) + (3x)(5)$$
$$= 12x^2 + 15x$$

1. $6c(5c + 3)$

2. $4m^2(-3m^3 + 2)$

3. $-5x^2(-3x + 1)$

4. $-m^2(6m^2 + n)$

5. $2y(4y^2 + 5y - 2)$

6. $-4a(-3a^2 + 2a - 5)$

7. $3x^5(x^4 - 2x^3 - x)$

8. $-2n^3(n^4 + 2n^3 - n^2 - n)$

9. $3a^2(-a^2b + b^2 - 6ab)$

10. $5x(-y^4 - xy^2 + 5x)$

Multiplying Binomials

Multiply.

Example:

$$
\begin{array}{cccc}
 & \text{First} & \text{Outside} & \text{Inside} & \text{Last}
\end{array}
$$

$$(x + 6)(x + 3) = x \bullet x + x \bullet 3 + 6 \bullet x + 6 \bullet 3$$

$$= x^2 + 3x + 6x + 18$$

$$\mathbf{= x^2 + 9x + 18}$$

FOIL method $\longrightarrow$ First Outside Inside Last

1. $(x + 3)(x - 3)$

2. $(x + 4)(x - 3)$

3. $(2x + 2)(x + 4)$

4. $(2a + 3)(4a + 2)$

5. $(x^2 + 2)(x + 1)$

6. $(3b + 4)(3b - 4)$

7. $(y^3 - 3)(y + 2)$

8. $(5x^2 + 4)(x - 4)$

9. $(4x^3 + x^2)(x^2 + x)$

10. $(3x^5 + 2x^2)(x^4 + 3x)$

Multiplying Polynomials

Multiply.

> **Example:** $(x - 2)(x^2 + x - 3)$
>
> $= x(x^2 + x - 3) - 2(x^2 + x - 3)$
>
> $= x^3 + x2 - 3x - 2x^2 - 2x + 6$
>
> $= x^3 - x^2 - 5x + 6$

1. $(m + 1)(m^2 - m + 3)$

2. $(2a - 1)(3a^2 - 2a - 1)$

3. $(x^2 - 3)(3x^2 - 4x + 2)$

4. $(n^3 - n^2)(n^3 - n^2 - n)$

5. $(x^2 - 2x + 1)(x^2 + x + 1)$

6. $(3m^3 - m^2 - 4)(3m^2 + 2m^2 + 5)$

Factoring Polynomials

Factor.

> **Example:**
>
> $$20x^3y^2 + 12xy^2 = 4xy^2(5x^2) + 4xy^2(3)$$
> $$= \mathbf{4xy^2(5x^2 + 3)}$$
>
> The common factor, $4xy^2$, was factored out.

1. $y^2 + 5y$

2. $4x^2 - 4x$

3. $17m^4 + 51m^3$

4. $4n^2 - 4n + 16$

5. $6x^2y + 3x^2y^2$

6. $5m^4n^4 - 3m^3n + 30n^3$

7. $a^9 + a^7 - a^4 - a^2 + a$

8. $5x^3y^2 - 15xy^3 + 20x^2y^2 - xy^2$

Factoring Trinomial Squares

Factor.

> **Example:**
>
> $x^2 + 8x + 16 = (x + 4)^2$
>
> A **trinomial square**, such as $x^2 + 8x + 16$, is the square of a binomial, $(x + 4)^2$.

1. $x^2 - 10x + 25$

2. $x^2 + 16x + 64$

3. $x^2 + 6x + 9$

4. $x^2 + 14x + 49$

5. $x^2 - 2x + 1$

6. $a^2 + 6ab + 9b^2$

7. $16x^2 - 40xy + 25y^2$

8. $9x^2 - 30x + 25$

9. $4x^4 + 16x^2 + 16$

10. $9x^4 - 6x^2y + y^2$

More Factoring

Factor.

Examples:

$$x^2 + 7x + 12 = \textbf{(x + 3)(x + 4)}$$

$$2x^2 - 22x + 60 = \textbf{2(x - 5)(x - 6)}$$

1. $x^2 - 8x + 15$

2. $x^2 + 10x + 24$

3. $x^2 - 4x - 45$

4. $x^2 + 11x + 28$

5. $x^2 - 14x + 45$

6. $x^2 + 10x + 21$

7. $x^2 - 21x - 100$

8. $2x^2 + 8x + 8$

9. $3x^2 - x - 4$

10. $4x^2 + 4x - 15$

Factoring to Solve Equations

Solve for x.

Example:

$$x^2 + x = 42$$

$$x^2 + x - 42 = 0$$

$$(x - 7)(x + 6) = 0$$

$$x - 7 = 0 \text{ or } x + 6 = 0$$

$$\mathbf{x = 7} \text{ or } \mathbf{x = {}^-6}$$

1. $x^2 - 3x - 28 = 0$

2. $x^2 + x - 12 = 0$

3. $x^2 + 6x - 27 = 0$

4. $x^2 + 5x = {}^-6$

5. $x^2 - 9x = {}^-14$

6. $2x^2 + 25x + 72 = 0$

7. $3x^2 = 27$

8. $3w^2 + 5w = {}^-2$

9. $6x^2 = 4x$

10. $3x^2 - 2x = 5$

Simplifying Rational Expressions

Simplify.

Example:

$$\frac{3x}{3x^2 + 3x} = \frac{3x}{3x(x + 1)} = \frac{1}{x + 1}$$

1. $\dfrac{6x + 24}{48x}$

2. $\dfrac{5y - 10}{5y}$

3. $\dfrac{3m - 12}{3m}$

4. $\dfrac{x^5 - x^4}{x^4 - x^3}$

5. $\dfrac{x + 8}{x^2 - 64}$

6. $\dfrac{x^2 - 1}{x + 1}$

7. $\dfrac{5x + 5}{x^2 + 7x + 6}$

8. $\dfrac{3x - 15}{5 - x}$

9. $\dfrac{x^2 - 1}{2x^2 - x - 1}$

10. $\dfrac{4x - 12}{6 - 2x}$

Multiplying Rational Expressions

Multiply. Simplify the product.

Example:

$$\frac{-3}{3x + 6} \cdot \frac{2}{x - 4} = \frac{-3 \cdot 2}{(3x - 6)(x - 4)}$$

$$= \frac{-3 \cdot 2}{3(x + 2)(x - 4)}$$

$$= \frac{-2}{(x + 2)(x - 4)}$$

1. $\dfrac{5a^2}{2} \cdot \dfrac{6}{10a^2}$

2. $\dfrac{3a}{b^2} \cdot \dfrac{4b}{9a^2}$

3. $\dfrac{x + 5}{2x} \cdot \dfrac{4x^3}{x + 5}$

4. $\dfrac{-3}{c} \cdot \dfrac{c^5}{c + 3}$

5. $\dfrac{x + 3}{x^2 - 2} \cdot \dfrac{x + 3}{x^2 - 9}$

6. $\dfrac{x - 3}{x - 4} \cdot \dfrac{x + 4}{x - 3}$

7. $\dfrac{4(x - 1)}{(x + 2)^2} \cdot \dfrac{x + 2}{(x - 1)^2}$

8. $\dfrac{x^2}{x^2 - 4} \cdot \dfrac{x^2 - 5x + 6}{x^2 - 3x}$

Dividing Rational Expressions

Divide. Simplify the quotient.

Example:

$$\frac{2x + 8}{6} \div \frac{x + 4}{12} = \frac{2x + 8}{6} \bullet \frac{12}{x + 4}$$

$$= \frac{2(x + 4)(12)}{6(x + 4)}$$

$$= 4$$

1. $\dfrac{3x^2}{8} \div \dfrac{6x}{5}$

2. $\dfrac{3}{x^5} \div \dfrac{9}{x^4}$

3. $\dfrac{6x^3}{7} \div 2x$

4. $\dfrac{4x - 4}{18} \div \dfrac{x - 1}{3}$

5. $\dfrac{4x - 8}{15} \div \dfrac{x - 2}{10}$

6. $\dfrac{x^2 - 1}{x} \div \dfrac{x - 1}{x + 1}$

7. $\dfrac{x^2 - 5x + 6}{x - 3} \div (x - 2)$

8. $\dfrac{x^2 - x - 20}{x^2 + 7x + 12} \div \dfrac{x^2 - 7x + 10}{x^2 + 10x + 24}$

Adding and Subtracting Rational Expressions

Add or subtract. Simplify.

Example:

$$\frac{x + 5}{x + 6} - \frac{3x - 7}{x + 6} = \frac{x + 5 - (3x - 7)}{x + 6}$$

$$= \frac{x + 5 - 3x + 7}{x + 6}$$

$$= \frac{2x + 12}{x + 6}$$

$$= {}^-2$$

1. $\dfrac{10m}{y} - \dfrac{8m}{y}$

2. $\dfrac{x + 4}{2x + 2} - \dfrac{3x}{2x + 2}$

3. $\dfrac{5a^2 - 3a + 2}{2a - 1} - \dfrac{3a^2 + 3a - 2}{2a - 1}$

4. $\dfrac{2x^2 - 13x + 8}{x + 4} + \dfrac{x^2 + 3x}{x + 4}$

5. $\dfrac{x^2 - 3x}{2x + 1} - \dfrac{3x^2 - 4x}{2x + 1}$

6. $\dfrac{{}^-3x^2 + 2x + 4}{5x + 1} + \dfrac{4x^2 + 2x - 3}{5x + 1}$

Solving Rational Equations

Solve each equation.

Example:

Multiply both sides by x, the Least Common Multiple (LCM).

$$x - \frac{5}{x} = {}^-4$$

$$x(x - \frac{5}{x}) = {}^-4(x)$$

$$x^2 - 5 = {}^-4x$$

$$x^2 + 4x - 5 = 0$$

$$(x + 5)(x - 1) = 0$$

$$x + 5 = 0 \text{ or } x - 1 = 0$$

$$\mathbf{x = {}^-5 \text{ or } x = 1}$$

1. $c + \dfrac{3}{c} = {}^-4$

2. $\dfrac{1}{6} + \dfrac{1}{5} = \dfrac{1}{x}$

3. $\dfrac{5}{b} + \dfrac{1}{2} = \dfrac{4}{b}$

4. $\dfrac{1}{6 - y} = \dfrac{1}{y}$

5. $\dfrac{3}{a + 2} = \dfrac{5}{a - 1}$

6. $\dfrac{x - 3}{3x + 2} = \dfrac{1}{5}$

7. $\dfrac{3x + 1}{3x - 2} = \dfrac{2x - 3}{2x + 2}$

8. $\dfrac{a - 1}{a + 1} = \dfrac{a - 2}{a - 3}$

Simplifying Radical Expressions

Simplify.

Examples:

$$\sqrt{x^2} = |x|$$

$$\sqrt{x^{12}} = \sqrt{x(x^6)^2} = x^6$$

$$\sqrt{9x^2} = \sqrt{3 \cdot 3 \cdot x^2 \cdot x^2 \cdot x}$$

$$= 3x^2\sqrt{x}$$

1. $\sqrt{16x^2}$

2. $\sqrt{(x-4)^2}$

3. $\sqrt{x^{10}}$

4. $\sqrt{x^{14}}$

5. $\sqrt{x^{15}}$

6. $\sqrt{25(x+5)^6}$

7. $\sqrt{12x^7}$

8. $\sqrt{225x^4y^3}$

9. $\sqrt{36x^5y^8}$

10. $\sqrt{(x+2)^{10}}$

Multiplying Radical Expressions

Multiply and simplify.

Examples:

$$\sqrt{3} \cdot \sqrt{27} = \sqrt{3 \cdot 27}$$
$$= \sqrt{81}$$
$$= \pm 9$$

$$\sqrt{5x} \cdot \sqrt{20x^2} = \sqrt{5x \cdot 20x^2}$$
$$= \sqrt{100x^3}$$
$$= \pm 10x \sqrt{x}$$

1. $\sqrt{5} \cdot \sqrt{15}$

2. $\sqrt{6} \cdot \sqrt{18x}$

3. $\sqrt{2x} \cdot \sqrt{18y}$

4. $\sqrt{7x} \cdot \sqrt{35y}$

5. $\sqrt{5} \cdot \sqrt{4x + 2}$

6. $\sqrt{2x^3} \cdot \sqrt{6x^3 y^6}$

7. $\sqrt{5x^2 y} \cdot \sqrt{10xy^2}$

8. $\sqrt{ab} \cdot \sqrt{ac}$

9. $\sqrt{x^{215}} \cdot \sqrt{y^{29}}$

10. $\sqrt{(x + 5)^6} \cdot \sqrt{(x + 5)^9}$

Dividing Radical Expressions

Divide and simplify.

Examples:

$$\frac{\sqrt{21}}{\sqrt{7}} = \sqrt{\frac{21}{7}} = \mathbf{\sqrt{3}}$$

$$\frac{\sqrt{8}}{\sqrt{2}} = \frac{8}{\sqrt{2}} \cdot \frac{\sqrt{2}}{\sqrt{2}}$$

$$= \frac{8\sqrt{2}}{2}$$

$$= \mathbf{4\sqrt{2}}$$

1. $\dfrac{\sqrt{16}}{\sqrt{25}}$

2. $\dfrac{\sqrt{1}}{\sqrt{4}}$

3. $\dfrac{\sqrt{18}}{\sqrt{3}}$

4. $\dfrac{\sqrt{15x^7}}{\sqrt{5x}}$

5. $\dfrac{\sqrt{45x^3}}{\sqrt{5x}}$

6. $\dfrac{2}{\sqrt{2}}$

7. $\dfrac{\sqrt{4}}{\sqrt{x}}$

8. $\dfrac{6x}{\sqrt{5}}$

Adding and Subtracting Radical Expressions

Add or subtract.

Examples:

$$2\sqrt{7} + 3\sqrt{7} = (2+3)\sqrt{7}$$
$$= 5\sqrt{7}$$

$$\sqrt{27} - \sqrt{3} = \sqrt{9 \cdot 3} - \sqrt{3}$$
$$= 3\sqrt{3} - 3$$
$$= 2\sqrt{3}$$

1. $3\sqrt{5} + 4\sqrt{5}$

2. $9\sqrt{2} - 5\sqrt{2}$

3. $8\sqrt{x} + 4\sqrt{x}$

4. $6\sqrt{8} + 2\sqrt{2}$

5. $\sqrt{20} + \sqrt{45}$

6. $\sqrt{80} - \sqrt{45}$

7. $\sqrt{4x} + \sqrt{9x^5}$

8. $\sqrt{8x + 8} + \sqrt{2x + 2}$

9. $\sqrt{x^9 - x^6} + \sqrt{4x^3 - 4}$

10. $\sqrt{3} - \sqrt{\dfrac{1}{3}}$

Equations with Radicals

Solve.

Example:
$$\sqrt{2x} - 5 = 9$$
$$\sqrt{2x} = 14$$
$$\left(\sqrt{2x}\right)^2 = (14)^2$$
$$2x = 196$$
$$\mathbf{x = 98}$$

1. $\sqrt{x} = 11$

2. $\sqrt{x} = 5.2$

3. $\sqrt{3x} - 6 = 2$

4. $\sqrt{x + 4} = 20$

5. $\sqrt{2x + 1} = 13$

6. $4 + \sqrt{x - 1} = 6$

7. $\sqrt{7x - 6} = \sqrt{x + 12}$

8. $\sqrt{5x - 4} = \sqrt{x + 16}$

Solving Quadratic Equations

Solve.

Examples:

$x^2 + 6x = 0$

$x(x + 6) = 0$

$x = 0$ or $x + 6 = 0$

$x = 0$ or **$x = -6$**

$x^2 - 2x - 8 = 0$

$(x - 4)(x + 2) = 0$

$x - 4 = 0$ or $x + 2 = 0$

$x = 4$ or **$x = -2$**

1. $x^2 + 7x = 0$

2. $4x^2 + 8x = 0$

3. $7x^2 - 3x = 0$

4. $5x^2 + 5x = 0$

5. $x^2 + 7x + 6 = 0$

6. $x^2 - 2x - 48 = 0$

7. $x^2 + 6x = {}^-9$

8. $3x^2 + 18x = {}^-15$

Solving Quadratic Equations by Completing the Square

Solve by completing the square.

Example:

$x^2 + 8x + 12 = 0$

$x^2 + 8x = -12$

$x^2 + 8x + 16 = -12 + 16$

$(x + 4)^2 = 4$

$\sqrt{(x + 4)^2} = \sqrt{4}$

$x + 4 = 2$ or $x + 4 = -2$

$\mathbf{x = -2}$ or $\mathbf{x = -6}$

A **coefficient** is the number in front of a variable in a term. For 5x, 5 is the coefficient.

To complete the square, take half of the x coefficient, square it, and add it to both sides.

Tip: Make sure the coefficient of x^2 is 1.

1. $x^2 + 14x = 15$

2. $x^2 - 7x - 2 = 0$

3. $x^2 + 8x + 15 = 0$

4. $x^2 - 2x - 10 = 0$

5. $x^2 + 2x - 5 = 0$

6. $2x^2 - 9x - 5 = 0$

7. $3x^2 - 2x - 5 = 0$

8. $6x^2 + 11x = 10$

The Quadratic Formula

Solve by using the quadratic formula.

The Quadratic Formula

For $ax^2 + bx + c = 0$,
the value of x is given by:

$$x = \frac{-b \pm \sqrt{b^2 - (4ac)}}{2a}$$

Example:

$$2x^2 + 7x = 4$$
$$2x^2 + 7x - 4 = 0$$
$$a = 2 \quad b = 7 \quad c = {}^-4$$

$$x = \frac{{}^-7 \pm \sqrt{7^2 - (4 \bullet 2 \bullet {}^-4)}}{2 \bullet 2}$$

$$x = \frac{{}^-7 \pm \sqrt{49 + 32}}{4}$$

$$x = \frac{{}^-7 + \sqrt{81}}{4} \text{ or } x = \frac{{}^-7 - \sqrt{81}}{4}$$

$$x = \frac{2}{4} \text{ or } x = \frac{{}^-16}{4}$$

$x = 2$ or $x = {}^-4$

1. $x^2 - 10x = {}^-22$

2. $3x^2 - 2x = 8$

3. $2x^2 + 5 = {}^-6x$

4. $2x^2 - 5x - 1 = 0$

Graphing Ordered Pairs

Plot the following points. The first one has been done for you.

A (-3,4)

1. B (5,0)

2. C (3,-2)

3. D (0,5)

4. E (-3,-4)

5. F (0,-3)

6. G (-1,1)

7. H (-4,0)

8. I (5,5)

9. J (3,2)

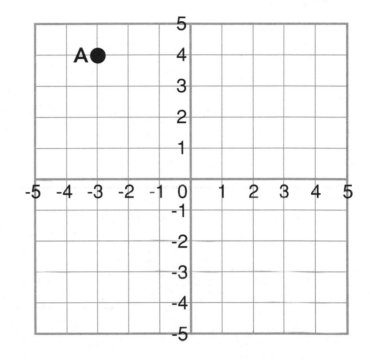

Graphing Linear Equations

Graph each linear equation using three points.

Example:

$3x + y = 2$
$y = {}^-3x + 2$

x	y
0	2
-1	5
1	-1

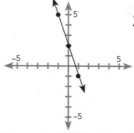

1. Solve the equation for y.

2. Substitute 0, -1, and 1 for x and find the corresponding values for y to make an ordered pair.

1. $y = x - 1$

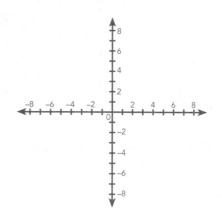

2. $y = 2x + 1$

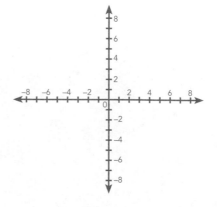

Graphing Using Intercepts

Graph each linear equation using the x- and y-intercepts.

Inserting 0 for y in a linear equation will yield the point where the line crosses the y-axis.

Inserting 0 for x in a linear equation will yield the point where the line crosses the x-axis.

Example:

$2y = 3x - 6$

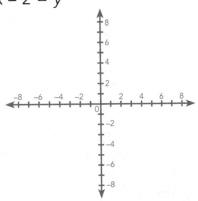

y-intercept	x-intercept
set x to 0	set y to 0
$2y = 3(0) - 6$	$2(0) = 3x - 6$
$2y = -6$	$6 = 3x$
$y = -3$	$x = 2$
(0,-3)	**(2,0)**

1. $x - 2 = y$

2. $3x + 1 = y$

Slope

Given two points, find the slope of each line.

Example:

$$\text{Slope: steepness of line} = \frac{\text{change in } y}{\text{change in } x}$$

$$(-5,2), (4,-1) = \frac{-1 - 2}{4 - (-5)} = \frac{-3}{9} = \frac{-1}{3}$$

1. (5,7), (4,0)

2. (2,1), (6,2)

3. (-1,7), (-4,9)

4. (1,10), (5,8)

5. (4,-1), (6,-5)

6. (-3,3), (5,-8)

7. (0,0), (-2,-8)

8. (2,7), (-3,-5)

Graphing Using the Slope-Intercept Form of an Equation

Graph each linear equation using the y-intercept and slope.

Example:

Slope-intercept form: $y = mx + b$,
where m = slope and b = y-intercept.

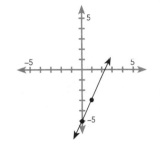

$y = 2x - 5$
y-intercept: $(0,\text{-}5)$
slope: 2

From the intercept, use the slope, $\dfrac{2}{1}$, to go 2 up and 1 to the right to get the second point for the line.

1. $y = \text{-}3x + 7$

2. $y = 2x - 4$

3. $y = \text{-}4x - 2$

4. $y + 3 = \text{-}x$

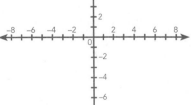

© Carson-Dellosa

The Slope-Intercept Form of an Equation

Write an equation for each line that contains the given point and has the given slope.

Slope-intercept form:
$y = mx + b$, where m = slope and b = y-intercept.

Find b by substituting the point and slope into the equation.

Example:

(3,6), $m = 1$

$6 = 1(3) + b$
$6 = 3 + b$
$b = 3$

$y = x + 3$

1. (-3,0), $m = -2$

2. (3,5), $m = 6$

3. (0,3), $m = -3$

4. (-2,1), $m = 3$

5. (-2,4), $m = \dfrac{-1}{2}$

6. (-2,1), $m = \dfrac{1}{2}$

The Point-Slope Form of an Equation

Write an equation for each line that contains the given pair of points.

Example:

Point-slope form: $y - y_1 = m(x - x_1)$, where m = slope and (x_1, y_1) = a point on the line.

Find the slope

$(\text{-}3, \text{-}2), (\text{-}1, 4)$

$\text{Slope} = \dfrac{4 - (\text{-}2)}{\text{-}1 - (\text{-}3)}$

$= \dfrac{6}{2}$

$= 3$

$y - y_1 = m(x - x_1)$

$y - (\text{-}2) = 3(x - (\text{-}3))$

$y + 2 = 3x + 9$

$y = 3x + 7$

1. (2,3), (-5,1)

2. (1,5), (3,2)

3. (0,0), (6,3)

4. (4,0), (0,-2)

5. (-2,6), (4,2)

6. (-4,0), (0,6)

Solving Systems of Equations: Graphing

Solve by graphing.

Example:

$y = 2x + 1$
$y + x = 4$

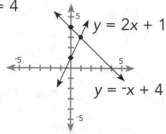

1. Graph both lines on the same graph.

2. Their intersection is the solution.

   The solution is **(1,3)**.

1. $y = -2x + 5$
   $2y = 5x + 10$

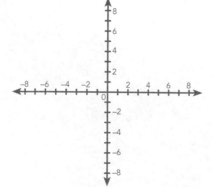

2. $x = y$
   $2x = y - 3$

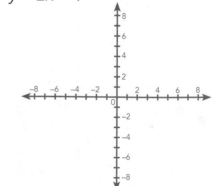

3. $x - 2y = 6$
   $2x - 3y = 5$

4. $y = 2x + 8$
   $y - 2x = 7$

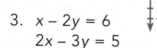

Solving Systems of Equations: The Substitution Method

Solve by using the substitution method.

Example:

$$y = 2x - 1$$
$$y = x + 2$$

Substitute $2x - 1$ for y in the second equation.

$$2x - 1 = x + 2$$
$$x = 3$$
$$y = 3 + 2$$
$$y = 5$$

Solve for x.
Plug x into either equation to solve for y.

The solution is **(3,5)**.

1. $y = -2x + 8$
   $y = x + 5$

2. $y = -4x - 5$
   $y = -2x + 10$

3. $x + y = -2$
   $x - y - 6$

4. $4x - 3y = 15$
   $x - 2y = 0$

5. $-2y + x = 8$
   $3y + 2x = 2$

6. $4x = 3 - y$
   $8x + 2y = 6$

Solving Systems of Equations: The Addition Method

Solve by using the addition method.

Example:

$$3x + 5y = -2$$
$$8x - 5y = -9$$

$$
\begin{array}{rcr}
3x + 5y &=& -2 \\
+8x - 5y &=& -9 \\
\hline
11x &=& -11 \\
x &=& -1
\end{array}
$$

Plug $x = -1$ into either equation to find y.

$$3(-1) + 5y = -2$$
$$-3 + 5y = -2$$
$$5y = 1$$
$$y = \frac{1}{5}$$

The solution is $(-1, \frac{1}{5})$.

1. $x + y = 3$
   $x - y = 7$

2. $-x + 2y = 7$
   $x + y = 8$

3. $x - 5y = -2$
   $7x + 5y = 18$

4. $4x + 3y = 7$
   $-4x + y = 5$

5. $5x - 2y = -3$
   $5x + 3y = 17$

6. $2x - 3y = -11$
   $5x - 2y = 0$

Linear Inequalities

Graph on a coordinate plane.

Example:

$y \leq x + 4$

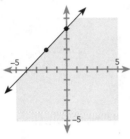

1. Graph the linear equation $y = x + 4$.

2. Use a solid line for $\leq$ or $\geq$ and a dashed line for $<$ or $>$.

3. Shade the area on the side of the line that makes the inequality true.

1. $y > {}^-x - 2$

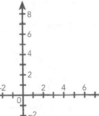

2. $y \geq x - 4$

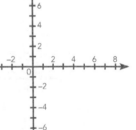

3. $y \leq {}^-2x + 4$

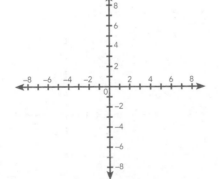

4. $x > 3$

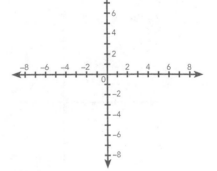

Graphing Systems of Linear Inequalities

Solve these systems by graphing.

Example:

$$y > x + 2$$
$$y > 3$$

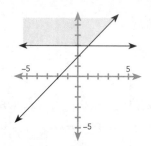

The region where the solutions (shading) is the solution.

1. $y > 3x - 1$
   $y < -2x + 3$

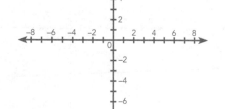

2. $y < 4x + 2$
   $y \geq -x + 1$

3. $y > 5$
   $2y > -x + 4$

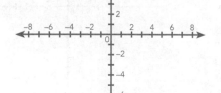

4. $x + y \leq 4$
   $y - x > 5$

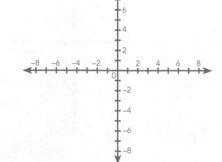

Using Equations

Solve each problem by using an equation.

1. Maria earned $2,300 more her second year on the job than her first. If she earned $29,100 her second year, what did she earn her first?

2. The dryers at the local laundromat cost 1 quarter for every 7 minutes. How many quarters will Blake have to use to dry 2 loads of laundry if each load takes 50 minutes to dry?

3. Jenny earned x amount of dollars babysitting Friday night. On Saturday night, she earned twice as much. If she earned $36 in total, how much did she earn the first night?

4. An artist sells each of his paintings for $50 at a craft show. How many did he sell at the show if he earned $1,850?

5. A roll of film costs $4.99. Each print costs $0.30 to develop. What is the total cost involved in buying and developing a roll of 36 exposures?

Using Proportions

Solve each problem by using a proportion.

1. A car travels 310 miles on 13 gallons of gasoline. How many gallons are needed to drive 475 miles?

2. A museum has a policy that 2 adults must accompany every group of 8 students. How many adults are needed to accompany 120 students to the museum?

3. The ratio of non-American-born students to American-born students at a school is 7 to 25. How many non-American-born students attend this school if 425 are American-born?

4. The scale on a map is 1 centimeter : 4.2 kilometers. If there are 12.5 centimeters between two cities on the map, what is the actual distance between the two cities?

5. The ratio of girls to boys in a school is 3:5. If there are 220 boys, what is the total number of students in the school?

6. It takes Brady twelve minutes to type two-thirds of a page. He is typing a seven-page term paper. If he continues at his present rate, how long total will it take him to finish his paper?

Make a Table

Solve each problem by making a table. Use a separate piece of paper.

1. A wealthy man donated money to his alma mater for a 10-year period. The first year he gave $1 million. The second year he gave $3 million. The third year he gave $5 million. If the pattern continued, how much money did he donate over a span of 10 years?

2. Shazia was offered two jobs when she graduated from college. One job had a starting salary of $19,000, with a guaranteed pay raise of $3,000 each year for 10 years. The other job had a starting salary of $27,000, with a guaranteed pay raise of $2,000 each year for 10 years. After 10 years which job would be paying more?

3. XYZ Company needs to increase their personnel due to record sales. In week number one, each of the original 25 employees hires and trains 2 new people. In week two, each of the new people hires and trains 2 new people. In week three, each of the newest employees hires and trains 2 new people. If the company continues this hiring trend over the next two months (eight weeks), how many employees will it have?

4. Stanley bought a car for $29,000. If it loses 10% of its value each year, what is the value of the car after 4 years?

Quantitative Comparisons

Compare the quantities in Column A with those in Column B, and choose from one of the four statements below.

A. The quantity in column A is greater.
B. The quantity in column B is greater.
C. The two quantities are equal.
D. The relationship cannot be determined.

	Column A	If...	Column B	
1.	$(a + 2)(a + 3)$	$a > 0$	$(a + 2)^2$	_____
2.	$\dfrac{1}{2}x$		$0.5x$	_____
3.	x	$x < y < 0$	$-3y$	_____
4.	xy	$x < y < z$	y^2	_____
5.	$4.0 \bullet 6{,}545$		$4.1 \bullet 6{,}545$	_____
6.	$a + b$	$ab > 0$	$a - b$	_____
7.	$\dfrac{a}{b}$	$\dfrac{a > 1}{b < 0}$	ab	_____

Working Backward

Solve each problem.

1. Aresia is thinking of a number. She divides her number by 8, squares it, then divides it by 3. Her result is 12. What number was Aresia thinking of?

2. Juan is thinking of a number. He halves it and then squares the result. He now has 2,401. What number was Juan thinking of?

3. Kami bought a new pack of graph paper for math class. She gave one quarter of the pack to Chang. Alexa got one fourth of what was left. Then Mario took one third of what was left. That left Kami with 36 sheets. How many sheets were in the pack of graph paper?

4. Michael is tall. Add 20 centimeters to his height and take a third of the sum. That gives you half of Roberto's height. Roberto is 150 centimeters tall. How tall is Michael?

5. Abigail bought a pair of jeans at a one-third-off sale. Abigail spent $14.30 for them. What was the original price of the jeans?

Using Logical Reasoning

Solve each problem.

1. Without computing, find the number that is the cube of 93:
   a. 804,958
   b. 805,643
   c. 804,357
   d. 804,872

2. It takes Maggie about 4 minutes to saw through a log. How long will it take her to saw the log into 4 pieces?

3. A company hired Ronnie and Ken as consultants. Together they made $14,500. If Ronnie had earned $500 less, both he and Ken would have been paid the same. How much were they each paid?

4. Five boys finished a race within 8 seconds of each other. Rick finished 1 second ahead of Craig, and Craig was not last. Sam finished 6 seconds before Taylor. Taylor finished 3 seconds behind Rick. Rick finished 5 seconds behind Brad. In what order did the boys finish?

5. Rachel, Robert, Charlotte, and Kevin were hired by the local rec league as coaches. Basketball, tennis, volleyball, and racquetball were the coaching positions. Robert's sister was hired to coach tennis. Neither Robert nor Kevin ever played volleyball or knew how to coach it. Charlotte had never learned to play tennis. Kevin disliked all sports that involved the use of a racket. Who was hired to coach which sport?

Using a Formula

Solve each problem.

1. A conference room is 20 feet long by 15 feet wide. Find the maximum amount of carpeting needed to cover the room's floor.

2. Find the distance traveled if you drive your car at an average speed of 55 mph for 8 hours. Use the formula $d = rt$ where d is distance, r is rate, and t is time.

3. A store pays $1,099 for a television and sells it for $2,199. If the store pays the salesman a $250 commission, how much profit is made by the store? Use the formula $P = I - E$ where P is profit, I is income, and E is expense.

4. Two buses leave a town at the same time going in opposite directions. One bus travels at 48 mph, and the other travels at 55 mph. In how many hours will they be 206 miles apart? Use the formula $d = rt$.

5. An airplane took 2 hours to fly 600 miles against a headwind. The return trip with a tailwind took $1\frac{2}{3}$ hours. Find the speed of the plane in the still air.

Using Percent

Solve each problem.

1. Anna's math test had 42 problems. She answered 37 correctly. What percent of the problems did she answer correctly?

2. A softball player had 40 hits in 150 turns at bat for the season. What percent of her turns at bat were hits?

3. The sales tax rate in Larry's state is 7%. How much tax would be charged on a purchase of $521.95? How much will the total cost of the purchase be?

4. Tasha's meal cost $21.04 before tax and tip. Calculate a 7% sales tax, and then calculate a 15% tip based on the cost before the sales tax. How much did Tasha's meal cost including the tax and tip?

5. Which is better, a discount of 20% or successive discounts of 10% and 10%?

Answer Key

Page 3
1. 125; 2. 21; 3. 96; 4. 7,776; 5. 3;
6. 248; 7. 80; 8. 30; 9. 100; 10. 4

Page 4
1. $x + 5$; 2. $5 - c$; 3. $10 + p$; 4. $3h$;
5. $\frac{y}{2}$ or $\frac{1}{2}(y)$; 6. $3n$; 7. $n + 3y$; 8. $y + y$ or
$2y$; 9. $2y - 3$; 10. $6y + 2$; 11. $\frac{n}{10}$; 12. $4s$

Page 5
1. $y = 7.2$; 2. $m = 349$; 3. $a = 113$;
4. $y = 287$; 5. $c = 1.64$; 6. $y = 4,946$;
7. $a = \frac{4}{7}$; 8. $p = \frac{13}{15}$; 9. $y = 4.66$;
10. $y = 284$

Page 6
1. $m = 7$; 2. $c = 6$; 3. $x = 0.66$;
4. $m = 372$; 5. $p = 61$; 6. $a = 16$;
7. $x = 236$; 8. $r = 0.96$; 9. $y = 5$;
10. $m = 0.4$

Page 7
1. $7n = 63$; $n = 9$,
2. $\$60h = \$42,720$; $h = 712$ hours
3. $12b = 5$; $b =$ about $\$0.42$
4. $t - 12 = 75$; $t = 87$ points
5. $324/2 = w$; $w = 162$ white golf balls
6. $56.25 + x = 70$; $x = \$13.75$

Page 8
1. 35; 2. 6.8; 3. 9; 4. 26; 5. 16;
6. 0; 7. -16, -13, 6, 14;
8. -33, -18, 0, 5;
9. -36, -34, -32, -28, -4;
10. -24, -14, -6, 6, 14

Page 9
1. $7x - 49$; 2. $-5y + 20$; 3. $3x - 6y$;
4. $-4x + 8y - 12$; 5. $18x - 24y + 48z$;
6. $-2.52x + 4.83y - 2.31$;
7. $-24x - 16y + 48$;
8. $12a - 15b + 21$;
9. $4x - 6y$; 10. $\frac{-5}{6}x + \frac{5}{12}y - 10$

Page 10
1. $4y$; 2. $-3x$; 3. $5a$; 4. $0.5m$;
5. $6x + 3y$; 6. $3y + 3z$;
7. $28a - 13b - 13c$; 8. $8p - 18$;
9. $\frac{3}{5}y + \frac{1}{5}x$; 10. $18a - 2b$

Page 11
1. $3y - 10$; 2. -5; 3. $-2b + 8$;
4. $6m + 5$; 5. $4y - 12$; 6. $8x - 5$;
7. $13y - 12x$; 8. $16a - b$;
9. 0; 10. $-x - 2y$

Page 12
1. $y = 9$; 2. $x = 11$; 3. $a = -7$;
4. $m = -11$; 5. $x = 11$; 6. $y = 11$;
7. $x = 21$; 8. $m = -2$; 9. $y = -8$;
10. $y = 13$

Page 13
1. $m = 14$; 2. $x = 1$; 3. $x = 2$;
4. $a = -1\frac{2}{3}$; 5. $b = 10$; 6. $m = 10$;
7. $y = 8\frac{2}{3}$; 8. $x = 5$; 9. $y = -8$;
10. $n = -8$

Page 14
1. $m = 7$ or $m = -7$;
2. $x = 5$ or $x = -5$;
3. $x = 18$ or $x = -18$;
4. $m = 7$ or $m = -7$;
5. $a = 7$ or $a = -7$;
6. $x = \frac{-1}{7}$ or $x = 1$;
7. $x = 16$ or $x = 4$;
8. $n = 7$ or $n = -1$;
9. $y = -3$ or $y = 2\frac{1}{4}$;
10. $x = -1$ or $x = 2$

Page 15
1. $y = -4$; 2. $y = 3$; 3. $x = 4$;
4. $x = -5$; 5. $b = 3$; 6. $m = 12$;
7. $y - 3$; 8. $p = -10$; 9. $x = 12$ or $x = -12$;
10. $m = -1$; 11. $y = -1$ or $y = \frac{1}{5}$;
12. $x = 2$ or $x = -8$

Page 16
1. a) 222; b) 54; c) 39; d) 19;
2. a) -1; b) 64; c) -125; d) $8m^3$;
3. a) 7; b) 6; c) 16; d) $x^2 + 2$

Page 17
1. $3x^2 - 8$; 2. $x^2 + 6x + 8$; 3. $3x - 2$
4. $9x^2 - 30x + 24$; 5. $3x + 4$;
6. $3x^2 + 1$

Answer Key

Page 18
1. $5x^3 - x^2 - 10x + 2$; 2. $x^2 + 3x - 2$;
3. $3x^3 - 6x$; 4. $^-x^2 + 5x + 1$;
5. 98; 6. $^-63$

Page 19
1. Function and 1-1
2. Function, not 1-1
3. Function and 1-1
4. Neither function nor 1-1

Page 20
1. $f^{-1}(x) = \frac{1}{4}x + 2$; 2. $f^{-1}(x) = \frac{1}{3}x - 2$;

3. $f^{-1}(x) = 2x + 2$; 4. $f^{-1}(x) = \frac{3}{2}x - 6$;

5. $f^{-1}(x) = \frac{4}{5(x + 3)}$; 6. $f^{-1}(x) = \sqrt[3]{x}$

Page 21
1. $r = \frac{d}{t}$; 2. $t = \frac{d}{r}$; 3. $p = \frac{I}{rt}$; 4. $r = \frac{I}{pt}$;
5. $\pi = \frac{A}{r^2}$; 6. $r^2 = \frac{A}{\pi}$; 7. $w = \frac{p - 2l}{2}$;
8. $r = \frac{C}{2\pi}$; 9. $b = \frac{2A}{h}$; 10. $m = \frac{E}{c^2}$

Page 22
1. $c = 13$; 2. $a = 7$; 3. $c = 4.24$;
4. $a = 28.28$; 5. $b = 20$; 6. $c = 17.89$

Page 23
1. $x > 7$; 2. $y \leq ^-21$; 3. $a < ^-19$;
4. $m \geq 0$; 5. $x > ^-1$; 6. $b \leq 9.2$;
7. $m < \frac{1}{9}$; 8. $c \geq \frac{1}{2}$; 9. $x < \frac{^-2}{9}$;
10. $m < 21$

Page 24
1. $x \geq ^-4$; 2. $m > ^-8$; 3. $y \geq 5$;
4. $p > ^-20$; 5. $x > \frac{^-1}{4}$; 6. $y \leq \frac{^-1}{8}$;
7. $x \leq ^-0.7$; 8. $n < ^-3$

Page 25
1. $x \leq 5$; 2. $x < ^-6$; 3. $y \leq ^-3$;
4. $x > ^-5$; 5. $m < ^-2\frac{1}{2}$; 6. $a \leq ^-4\frac{1}{3}$;
7. $x < 1\frac{4}{5}$; 8. $b > 2$; 9. $m > 25$;
10. $x \geq ^-3$

Page 26
1. $y > 9$;

2. $x \leq 5$;

3. $c \geq ^-6$;

4. $m \geq 3$;

Page 27
1. 3^9; 2. 9^{15}; 3. $(^-5)^7$; 4. x^{13}; 5. y^{13};
6. m^3; 7. x^5y^{10}; 8. $3^2a^6b^8$; 9. $b^7c^6d^2$;
10. $2^2x^4y^4$; 11. m^6n^{10}; 12. $x^4y^3z^5$

Page 28
1. 6^4; 2. 4^4; 3. n; 4. x^3; 5. a^3; 6. m^4n^3;
7. a; 8. $4x^3$; 9. x^3y^2; 10. $5a^2$

Page 29
1. $\frac{1}{4^3}$; 2. $\frac{1}{5^4}$; 3. $\frac{1}{m^6}$; 4. $\frac{1}{(3y)^2}$; 5. $\frac{7}{n^4}$; 6. $\frac{c}{d^5}$;
7. 256; 8. m^{32}; 9. $16t^4$; 10. $27x^6$;
11. $\frac{4}{a^4}$; 12. $\frac{a^3b^6}{c^3}$

Page 30
1. ^-12y; 2. $^-x^2$; 3. m^2; 4. $8p^7$;
5. $^-y^8$; 6. $30n^6$; 7. a^5b^5; 8. $^-27x^4y^5$;
9. $^-16m^6n^6$; 10. $^-48c^6$

Page 31
1. m^3; 2. $\frac{3}{2}x$; 3. b^5; 4. $\frac{4}{c^3}$; 5. $^-4x^5$;
6. $^-4$; 7. $^-m^5$; 8. $^-8y^5$; 9. $^-\frac{5}{7}m^5n^4$;
10. $^-4a^5$

Page 32
1. $^-13y^3 + 2y - 32$; 2. $7n^3 - n - 8$;
3. $11y^2 - 4$; 4. $5c^4$; 5. $5x^3 + 3xy^2$;
6. $^-15a^2b^2 - 2ab$; 7. $^-7xy^2 + 5xy$;
8. $m^3 + m^2n^2 - m^2 - 2$; 9. $3x^2y$

Page 33
1. $a^2 + 6a$
2. $32y^4 + 4y^2 + y$
3. $4m^5 + 13m^2 + 5m - 3$
4. $^-x^3 + 7x^2 + x - 10$
5. $10x^7 + 6x^5 - 10x^4 + 8x^2 + 2$
6. $^-2m^4n^3 + 6m^3n^3 + 2mn^2 - 2m^2 + 9$

Answer Key

Page 34
1. $2a^4 + 6$;
2. $-5x^3 + 4x^2 + 3x + 12$;
3. $8y^3 - 8y^2 - 5y + 16$;
4. $9m^3 + 3m^2 + 2m - 1$;
5. $6x^4 - 5x^3 + 5x - 4$;
6. $-5t^5 + 8t^4 - 3t^2 + 3t + 1$;
7. $3y^3 - 2y^2 - 2y + 2$;
8. $n^5 + 5n^4 + 2n^3 + 14n + 3$;
9. $7ab^5 + b^4 + ab^4 - 4ab^3 + 3b^2 + 1$

Page 35
1. $30c^2 + 18c$; 2. $-12m^5 + 8m^2$;
3. $15x^3 - 5x^2$; 4. $-6m^4 - m^2n$;
5. $8y^3 + 10y^2 - 4y$;
6. $12a^3 - 8a^2 + 20a$;
7. $3x^9 - 6x^8 - 3x^6$;
8. $-2n^7 - 4n^6 + 2n^5 + 2n^4$
9. $-3a^4b + 3a^2b^2 - 18a^3b$,
10. $-5xy^4 - 5x^2y^2 + 25x^2$

Page 36
1. $x^2 - 9$; 2. $x^2 + x - 12$;
3. $2x^2 + 10x + 8$ 4. $8a^2 + 16a + 6$;
5. $x^3 + x^2 + 2x + 2$; 6. $9b^2 - 16$;
7. $y^4 + 2y^3 - 3y - 6$;
8. $5x^3 - 20x^2 + 4x - 16$;
9. $4x^5 + 5x^4 + x^3$;
10. $3x^9 + 11x^6 + 6x^3$

Page 37
1. $m^3 + 2m + 3$; 2. $6a^3 - 7a^2 + 1$;
3. $3x^4 - 4x^3 - 7x^2 + 12x - 6$;
4. $n^6 - 2n^5 + n^3$; 5. $x^4 - x^3 - x + 1$;
6. $15m^5 - 5m^4 + 15m^3 - 25m^2 - 20$

Page 38
1. $y(y + 5)$; 2. $4x(x - 1)$
3. $17m^3(m + 3)$; 4. $4(n^2 - n + 4)$
5. $3x^2y(2 + y)$
6. $n(5m^4n^3 - 3m^3 + 30n^2)$
7. $a(a^8 + a^6 - a^3 - a + 1)$
8. $xy^2(5x^2 - 15y + 20x - 1)$

Page 39
1. $(x - 5)^2$; 2. $(x + 8)^2$; 3. $(x + 3)^2$;
4. $(x + 7)^2$; 5. $(x - 1)^2$; 6. $(a + 3b)^2$;
7. $(4x - 5y)^2$; 8. $(3x - 5)^2$;
9. $(2x^2 + 4)^2$; 10. $(3x^2 - y)^2$

Page 40
1. $(x - 3)(x - 5)$; 2. $(x + 6)(x + 4)$;
3. $(x - 9)(x + 5)$; 4. $(x + 7)(x + 4)$;
5. $(x - 9)(x - 5)$; 6. $(x + 7)(x + 3)$;
7. $(x - 25)(x + 4)$; 8. $2(x + 2)^2$;
9. $(3x - 4)(x + 1)$; 10. $(2x + 5)(2x - 3)$

Page 41
1. $x = 7$ or $x = {}^-4$; 2. $x = {}^-4$ or $x = 3$;
3. $x = {}^-9$ or $x = 3$; 4. $x = {}^-2$ or $x = {}^-3$;
5. $x = 7$ or $x = 2$; 6. $x = {}^-8$ or $x = \frac{{}^-9}{2}$;
7. $x = {}^-3$ or $x = 3$; 8. $w = {}^-1$ or $w = \frac{{}^-2}{3}$;
9. $x = 0$ or $x = \frac{2}{3}$; 10. $x = {}^-1$ or $x = \frac{5}{3}$

Page 42
1. $\frac{x + 4}{8x}$; 2. $\frac{y - 2}{y}$; 3. $\frac{m - 4}{m}$; 4. x;
5. $\frac{1}{x - 8}$; 6. $x - 1$; 7. $\frac{5}{x + 6}$; 8. ${}^-3$;
9. $\frac{x + 1}{2x + 1}$; 10. ${}^-2$

Page 43
1. $\frac{3}{2}$; 2. $\frac{4}{3ab}$; 3. $2x^2$; 4. $\frac{{}^-3c^4}{c + 3}$;
5. $\frac{x + 3}{(x^2 - 2)(x - 3)}$; 6. $\frac{x + 4}{x - 4}$;
7. $\frac{4}{(x + 2)(x - 1)}$; 8. $\frac{x}{x + 2}$

Page 44
1. $\frac{5x}{16}$; 2. $\frac{1}{3x}$; 3. $\frac{3x^2}{7}$; 4. $\frac{2}{3}$; 5. $\frac{8}{3}$;
6. $\frac{(x + 1)^2}{x}$; 7. 1; 8. $\frac{(x + 6)(x + 4)}{(x + 3)(x - 2)}$

Page 45
1. $\frac{2m}{y}$; 2. $\frac{{}^-x + 2}{x + 1}$; 3. $\frac{2a^2 - 6a + 4}{2a - 1}$;
4. $\frac{3x^2 - 10x + 8}{x + 4}$; 5. $\frac{{}^-2x^2 + x}{2x + 1}$;
6. $\frac{x^2 + 4x + 1}{5x + 1}$

Page 46
1. $c = {}^-3$ or $c = {}^-1$; 2. $x = \frac{30}{11}$;
3. $b = {}^-2$; 4. $y = 3$; 5. $a = \frac{{}^-13}{2}$;
6. $x = \frac{17}{2}$; 7. $x = \frac{4}{21}$; 8. $a = \frac{5}{3}$

Answer Key

Page 47

1. $4|x|$; 2. $|x - 4|$; 3. x^5; 4. x^7;

5. $x^7\sqrt{x}$; 6. $5(x + 5)^3$; 7. $2x^3\sqrt[3]{3x}$;

8. $15x^2 y\sqrt{y}$; 9. $6x^2y^4\sqrt{x}$; 10. $(x + 2)^5$

Page 48

1. $5\sqrt{3}$; 2. $6\sqrt{3x}$; 3. $6\sqrt{xy}$; 4. $7\sqrt{5xy}$;

5. $\sqrt{20x + 10}$; 6. $2x^3y^3\sqrt{3}$; 7. $5xy\sqrt{2xy}$;

8. $a\sqrt{bc}$; 9. $x^{107}y^{14}\sqrt{xy}$; 10. $(x + 5)^7\sqrt{x + 5}$

Page 49

1. $\frac{4}{5}$; 2. $\frac{1}{2}$; 3. $\sqrt{6}$; 4. $x^3\sqrt{3}$; 5. $3x$;

6. $\sqrt{2}$; 7. $\frac{2\sqrt{x}}{x}$; 8. $\frac{6x\sqrt{5}}{5}$

Page 50

1. $7\sqrt{5}$; 2. $4\sqrt{2}$; 3. $12\sqrt{x}$; 4. $14\sqrt{2}$;

5. $5\sqrt{5}$; 6. $\sqrt{5}$; 7. $(3x^2 + 2)\sqrt{x}$;

8. $3\sqrt{2x + 2}$; 9. $(x^3 + 2)\sqrt{x^3 - 1}$;

10. $\frac{2}{3}\sqrt{3}$ or $\frac{2\sqrt{3}}{3}$

Page 51

1. $x = 121$; 2. $x = 27.04$; 3. $x = \frac{64}{3}$;

4. $x = 396$; 5. $x = 84$; 6. $x = 5$; 7. $x = 3$;

8. $x = 5$

Page 52

1. $x = 0$ or $x = {}^-7$; 2. $x = 0$ or $x = {}^-2$;

3. $x = 0$ or $x = \frac{3}{7}$; 4. $x = 0$ or $x = {}^-1$;

5. $x = {}^-6$ or $x = {}^-1$; 6. $x = 8$ or $x = {}^-6$;

7. $x = {}^-3$; 8. $x = {}^-5$ or $x = {}^-1$

Page 53

1. $x = 1$ or $x = {}^-15$;

2. $x = \frac{7}{2} + \sqrt{14.25}$ or $x = \frac{7}{2} - \sqrt{14.25}$

3. $x = {}^-3$ or $x = {}^-5$;

4. $x = 1 + \sqrt{11}$ or $x = 1 - \sqrt{11}$;

5. $x = {}^-1 + \sqrt{6}$ or $x = {}^-1 - \sqrt{6}$;

6. $x = 5$ or $x = \frac{{}^-1}{2}$; 7. $x = \frac{5}{3}$ or $x = {}^-1$;

8. $x = \frac{2}{3}$ or $x = \frac{{}^-5}{2}$

Page 54

1. $x = 5 \pm \sqrt{3}$; 2. $x = \frac{{}^-4}{3}$ or $x = 2$

3. no real solutions; 4. $x = \frac{5 \pm \sqrt{33}}{4}$

Page 55

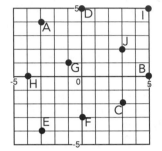

Page 56

1.   2.

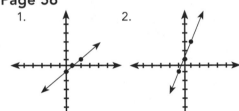

Page 57

1.   2.

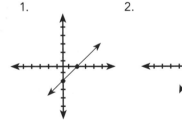

Page 58

1. 7; 2. $\frac{1}{4}$; 3. $\frac{{}^-2}{3}$; 4. $\frac{{}^-1}{2}$;

5. $^-2$; 6. $\frac{{}^-11}{8}$; 7. 4; 8. $\frac{12}{5}$

Answer Key

Page 59

1.

2.

3.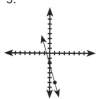

4.

Page 60

1. $y = {}^{-}2x - 6$; 2. $y = 6x - 13$;
3. $y = {}^{-}3x + 3$; 4. $y = 3x + 7$;
5. $y = \frac{-1}{2}x + 3$; 6. $y = \frac{1}{2}x + 2$

Page 61

1. $y = \frac{2}{7}x + \frac{17}{7}$; 2. $y = \frac{-3}{2}x + \frac{13}{2}$;
3. $y = \frac{1}{2}x$; 4. $y = \frac{1}{2}x - 2$;
5. $y = \frac{2}{3}x + \frac{14}{3}$; 6. $y = \frac{3}{2}x + 6$

Page 62

1. (0,5)

2. (-3,-3)

3. (-8,-7)

4. There is no
solution; the lines
are parallel.

Page 63

1. (1,6); 2. $(\frac{-15}{2}, 25)$; 3. (2,-4);
4. (6,3); 5. (4,-2); 6. Infinitely many
solutions

Page 64

1. (5,-2); 2. (3,5); 3. $(2, \frac{4}{5})$; 4. $(\frac{-1}{2},3)$;
5. (1,4); 6. (2,5)

Page 65

1.

2.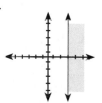

3.

4.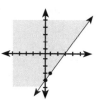

Page 66

1.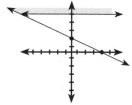

2.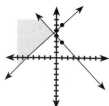

3.

4.

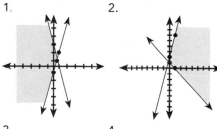

Answer Key

Page 67

1. $x + 2{,}300 = 29{,}100$; $x = \$26{,}800$
2. $\frac{50}{7} \cdot 2 = x$; $x = $ about 16 quarters (8 quarters for each load);
3. $x + 2x = 36$; $x = \$12.00$;
4. $50x = 1{,}850$; $x = 37$ paintings
5. $4.99 + 0.30(36) = c$; $c = \$15.79$

Page 68

1. $\frac{13}{310} = \frac{x}{475}$; $x = $ about 20 gallons;
2. $\frac{2}{8} = \frac{x}{120}$; $x = 30$ adults;
3. $\frac{7}{25} = \frac{x}{425}$; $x = 119$ students;
4. $\frac{1}{4.2} = \frac{12.5}{x}$; $x = 52.5$ km;
5. $\frac{3}{5} = \frac{x}{220}$; $132 + 220 = 352$ students;
6. $\frac{18}{1} = \frac{x}{7}$; $x = 126$ minutes or 2 hours, 6 minutes

Page 69

1. $100 million
2. the $19,000/year job
3. 12,775 employees
4. $19,026.90

Page 70

1. A; 2. C; 3. B; 4. D; 5. B; 6. D; 7. A

Page 71

1. 48; 2. 98; 3. 96 sheets; 4. 205 cm;
5. $21.45

Page 72

1. c; 2. 12 minutes
3. Ronnie: $7,500; Ken: $7,000
4. Brad, Sam, Rick, Craig, Taylor
5. Rachel—tennis; Charlotte—volleyball; Robert—racquetball; Kevin—basketball

Page 73

1. 300 sq. feet; 2. 440 miles;
3. $850; 4. 2 hours; 5. 330 mph

Page 74

1. 88%; 2. 27%; 3. $36.54; $558.49
4. total cost: $25.67; 5. 20%